BILL O'REALLY!

Donald Gorbach

ISBN-10 1981510087
ISBN-13 978-1981510085

"AND GUYS, IF YOU EXPLOIT A GIRL, IT WILL COME BACK TO GET YOU. THAT'S CALLED KARMA!"

— BILL O'REILLY